T0088891

Revolution
Struggle Poems

Tendai R. Mwanaka

Langaa Research & Publishing CIG
Mankon, Bamenda

Publisher

Langaa RPCIG
Langaa Research & Publishing Common Initiative Group
P.O. Box 902 Mankon
Bamenda
North West Region
Cameroon
Langaagrp@gmail.com
www.langaa-rpcig.net

Distributed in and outside N. America by African Books Collective
orders@africanbookscollective.com
www.africanbookscollective.com

ISBN: 9956-762-13-X

About the Poet

Tendai. R. Mwanaka is a multidisciplinary artist from Chitungwiza, Zimbabwe. His work touches on essays, non-fictions, poetry, plays, fictions, music, sound art, photography, drawings, paintings, collage, video, mixed media, inter genres, inter disciplines. *Voices from Exile,* a poetry collection on Zimbabwe's political situation and exile in South Africa came out from Lapwing Publications, Northern Ireland, 2010, *Keys in the River,* a novel of interlinked short fictions came out from Savant Books and Publications, 2012, *Zimbabwe: The Blame Game,* a book of creative non-fiction on Zimbabwe came out from Langaa, 2013. *Zimbabwe: The Urgency of Now* came from Langaa, 2015, *A Dark Energy* will come from Aignos Publishing Inc. His work has been published in over 300 journals, anthologies and magazines in over 27 countries. He has been nominated, shortlisted and won some prizes and some of his work has been translated into French and Spanish.

Table of Contents

Acknowledgements

1. The Tunisian Revolution
2. White Girl, Black Boy
3. The Egyptian Revolution
4. The War
5. The Libyan War
6. A Portfolio Of Defiance
7. The Ivory Coast War
8. Stations Of The Cross
9. The Real Nuclear Threat
10. Sexually Transmitted Leadership
11. Ceaser's Breathe
12. Team Israel
13. Team Palestine
14. The Middle East Game
15. Perpetuating 1967
16. Nazi Israel
17. I Am Going To Marry Her
18. The Rush To Own
19. Infinity
20. Doing A Camus
21. Fundamentalism
22. Is This The "Next Rwanda"?
23. Every God
24. Karma's "Shoe" List
25. Undying Echoes
26. A Text For Haiti
27. Licking Wounds
28. Murphy's Un-Thought

29. Somalia, "The Death Walk"
30. Untitled
31. Euro Burning
32. The Shadow Now Gone
33. Fermi's Paradox
34. Us Grand Political Theatre
35. For The Mullahs In Iran
36. He Was Never Free
37. Syrian Unrest
38. We Had No Right To Be There
39. We Dont Need Another War: Not Iran!
40. An Enermy Inside
41. 2.5 Years Of Obamania (Less)
42. Nobel Prize 2009
43. Revolution: The Sparrow's Fall
44. The King's Burden
45. Is The Remainder Of The Way So Long?
46. Gadaffism: Gone
47. Autumn
48. Revolution Re-Focussing
49. It Took A Judas
50. Bahrain/Yemen/Saudi Arabia- The Music Of The Triangle
51. A Text For Baga
52. ECB vs. The Federal Reserve: Dead Wood Institutions
53. Squatter Slums
54. Corporatism Vs People: Occupy Wall Street
55. The Benched Refugee
56. Bibi Aisha Of Afghanstan
57. Pretty This Grief
58. Terror War: Through The Eyes Of Bush And Chaney

59. Saying What's Already SAID
60. Drone Attacks

Acknowledgements

Some of these poems or pieces of have first appeared in the following among other magazines, blogs, anthologies and journals:

Off the Coast, Children, churches and daddies and anthologies, Pacific journal Struggle Magazine, Spittoon Magazine, Jenny Magazine, Ginger Piglet Magazine, BLUEPAPER, Deadsnakes, The Blue Hour, Mojoportal, Earthbourne Journal, Calvary cross, Novaim and Napalm, ShotGlass Journal, MelBrake Press, Both Sides Now, Black Magnolis Literary Journal, Squawk Back, Puff Puff Anthology vol 2, Pluck, Poet's stage, Full of Crow, Bursting and Droning mag, The Tower Journal, Fowl Run Press, Exercise Bowler, The Bitchin Kirtsch, Bewildering Stories, Fowl Pox, The New Verse News, Decanto, The Phoenix review poetry magazine, Poetrymonthlyinternational, Numinous spiritual magazine, Inclement, Neverbuy poetry, Exiled Ink magazine, Pennine platform, The Red Wheelbarrow, The Delinquent, Neonhighway, Pulsar, New Coin, Poems for Bangui blog by Wakhoka Wanjohi, Poems for Haiti anthology, For Rhino in a Shrinking World International Anthology 2012, Conscious Magazine, Poetry Bulawayo, More Than a Number Anthology, The Muse- An International Anthology, SCWI ournal, ventsalizes; Eastlit mag, Malaysian Poetic Chronicles.

The Tunisian Revolution

It started with Mohamed Bouziz, gunning an unstoppable bullet with his death. He was 26, married, married with children. Had a university degree, couldn't find employment. Had a market place, was a hawker, selling. Had his things confiscated by a woman police. He protested and she slapped him, the humiliation of it all! An Arab woman slapping an Arab man, is unthinkable? He tried to pursue the case with the authorities, they ignored his complaint. He committed suicide, electrocuting himself, the speaking protest, a tidy rhythm. This suicide started humming, like winter metal. Tunisia exploded and Bennali was kicked out, creating debate leaf-shaped points, across the Arab world....The Arab world: is now a boiling pot... One country after another, each, a long Moor's hour, from unriboning decades of dictatorships.

White Girl, Black Boy

The human skin is now the only existing surface
That has survived a history of cut and paste manifest destiny
The dermis has become an interlocutor of presenting, as a
surface
It both jails, skyrockets the contours of the landscape and
flesh

I imagine, imagining my imaginations
What if white is not?
Really white!
A smudgy pinkish colour?

The black boy thinks: If I was really black, I might not really
be seen
Because I could hide things in my own blackness and if she
were really white
When she is being white, white as family tree white
She wouldn't see me, for she would only be the wind
Light stripes of wind, pinned around my corporeal clothes
Like cold tasting light, itself in the mouth of itself

The white girl thinks: It is a black skin muddled, annihilated
of its truth
No more his own skin; crythematous-patches, necrotic
tissues-indurated
Skin boiling in its blackness
The black thing always, wanting, needling…
Getting in the way,
Even now

Like the deadly white of the sky
She inherited the whiteness
The sugar coating whiteness
It is whiteness
As witness

She thinks, and you can't deny her that: This is the fire
injected by history into my veins.
A white horned hunger to live, as long as bacteria
In this whiteness
Whiteness as white-coloured white?

The two, the white girl and the black boy, are talking of the
cloudy of ice-cold that is always hovering on either side of
this harness, the weave is the skin, which attempts to harness
a centrality of spirit, and the rituals each of the two enacts to
cipher it out in their relationship.
But, I will do an Alice walker here
And I imagine, with Walker, the psychic liberation of black if
it understands
Black is not really black
I imagine, still with Walker, the exhilarating feeling of white if
it could walk (doing a Walker with me) away from the caged
feeling
Of its body, in its own skins

The Egyptian Revolution

Young babies, young children, young people out welling, youngling, unwarping. Christians and Muslims taking us to the edge of intention and showing us what lies beyond doubt? Old men down warping, fathers and mothers. The Israeli press called them stray dogs. But the figures kept ballooning. It started with tens of thousands, then hundreds of thousands, then millions... Cairo is bustling; a mass mortality horizon, Alexandria and Monsouri city are swamped. Tahrir, the liberation square is the hub of this monsoon chanting

"The nation wants the ouster of the regime."

The day's song is a lament drawn out like a final breath lost in the stars. It's millions wearing the country's flag as if the pharaohs have thumped every other country at the CAF African nations cup to win it again. Jubilant, passionate, angry... It is a carnival atmosphere. It is a nation raising its bread, the symbol of its suffering and hunger. It is a nation crucifying effigies of its napoleon. It is a nation waving placards written with the fine point of their anger and pain

"Mubarak go to hell"
"America butt out"
"Tel Aviv is mourning"
"Mubarak leave-
we want to live."

They name the forms of control, youths screaming for an open road to somewhere. Over 30 years of mis-governance, human rights abuses, curfews..., suffering. It is over 30 years

4

n which America and Israel ruled by robot controlling Mubarak. Giving the top brass of army and security the loot of the 2 billion dollars, American taxpayer's money: just to protect Israel. Israel would joke

"We have one person controlling 80 plus millions of enemies."

Now she has got to face the 80 plus million enemies across its borders. Israel is a bubbling "spoilt" child, afraid, scared....

The War

I have decided to leave this city of war. The war has gone out
of control. You never know who belongs to whom,
anymore. What the fight is all about!
The war is still dragging on its
fiery tail through the
dead city like
some
giant prehistoric creature. I take a maze of trail, which threads
its way out of the city, through the unchecked growth
and rubbish. I keep walking, leaving the images
of the city, into the wilderness. The sky
is layers of cotton-thick smoke.
Wild, cross-bred thorny
roses, scraggly
Aloe
plants, hollyhocks, and emaciated chrysanthemums dotes the
trail. Sprigs of tamarisk, sprigs of furze, herbs still
exuding scents, the grass is singing dirges
around my feet, as I pass between
air's legs, it snakes a hiss,
a bark. I begin to see,
to feel another
war
in these species difficult and deeper into great piles of life
fomenting. An irresistible occasion, this garland of
demonstrations! Morning glories, their
purple flowers look down on the
melee much as generals
observe their wars
whilst others

are

doing the actual fighting. These generals are the ravishment
of their own extending success, a display. The wheat fields
weaving brushstrokes of their pride, they dance
and shout as of people of a ceaselessly
bombed city when it's freed.
Rose bushes poised
like ballerinas,

a

choreography which gathers them in front of the
forsythia. Quack grass, thistle, cockleburs and
black eyed Susan: are the privates,
sergeants, lieutenants,
and captains;
fighting
the
war for the generals; the morning glories. This war does not
pace itself, space itself…, for it is self contained in itself

The Libyan war

Before even the first protest was drawn out, there were the killings for years and years. Gadaffi, the giraffe, that fringed phylactory-bound, son of a prophet has now taken the whole country into ransom, pelting his people with bullets, bombing whole towns into rubble, his needles of bullets pointing eastwards.

For many years he had guts and beauty, an intellect that despised the humanist pretensions of the West, its white-skinned predacity. He could smell the corruptions of empires, the annihilations of naked creatures. He was brother man to the revolutions, but now he is being absorbed by his own medicine, the sulphuric acid melting him.

Praying for light and air- a darkness approaching he had never sensed before, he has developed a white finger. Now his western finger- his white friends- are in this war against him. Such ill-conceived wars are just what they usually need for the roar of that unreasonable action. Boom!

East is revolutionary, the uprising, the wars for towns, adding to strategic places? NATO (rather the: *Not Asked To Overstay* organisation), the de-facto UN of the west, is at its games again, carving their own cake in Libya. They want the ouster of Gadaffi, bombing, as usual, innocent people and towns into rubble or collateral damage, that clever American coinage of terms...

Even though I don't subscribe to NATO's ulterior motives of invading other countries without a by-your –leave, but 41

8

years under one dictator is far worse than NATO's games minus those stupid killings. At least NATO won't stay (overstay) for that long. It told us so! And we are always so stupid to believe?

But Gadaffi has to realise as soon as possible that a man who lacks the means to an end is headed towards a shapeless wilderness. That if you are a king, never undresses your minors. He should ask Mubarak, Bennali..? Now the modern pharaoh is bedridden, facing a death penalty, creating beautiful soap for us whilst Bennali enjoys Saudi's banquets. Too bad!

Gadaffi should know that too often self-induced addictions to grand delusions cause a man to plot his own undoing. Ask the British, Soviet Union, Byzantine became Ottoman Turkey, Alexander the fool, and now America…

But NATO or Gadaffi answers, both are not the answers to Libya. The revolutionaries (NTC) might be the way to the answer. But, for most of us, the liberty to interpret, to think about it all is frightening. Is this new baby a darling or a stranger?

The answer is: It should always be about the people….

A Portfolio of Defiance

I am stretching out my wings
Winging away to the mountain of promise, potential
With every right to hope
I am taking this shape, you could shape, too
….it's a saying, or is it musical?
I need to survive the thunderstorms and be a new rose
Spewing perfume, blooming…
With every right to hope

The fires are still doing, negotiating
Black veins stuffed with hope
Dreams, angers; a soul
Of undeterred definitions of scope

No clocks, I know what time it is
The manure pilled around my bones, one day
Will become the garden that I ought to be
But in the meanwhile I put in the work and dreamed I will
succeed

I have clenched a coal hot October sun in my being; carry it
in my throat,
dry, accumulating pain, hot, burnt…
Want of a horizon of water, knowing it would boil me
A pocket of it might do, maybe moistening me
Maybe, I will pour out a steaming pot, steeped with
smouldering of positivity

I weave constellations (galaxies that think rhapsody) from
memory, the Milky Way blued into the loom with fainting
threads
I burn the stars with my cold breath, the sloshing, steaming
sounds of burnt stones, immersed in water

I have found threads of meaning in this existence
Ropes without meaning
I have opened out these threads, with my mouth
I have tied everything to these threads, unthreading the ropes,
everything
All at once

I incline towards complexity spaced seriality of life units
I will be the tallest person on top of the mountain
The grown up

A bird with its river flows
The bird, breaking the sky, effortlessly
The lark's amplitude, disintensive
Up and up it feels, it says, it is free
O, ohohoh, I am the lark, ohohoh
In my intensive disintensiveness
My brain humming with infrasonic success!

The Ivory Coast war

Quattara and Gagbgo are the fighting gods. It's the Ivorian phenomena, again and again. It's the geometry found in the shape of their living. It happened in year 2000 and now it's back again. It's the fate they have always chosen, and live in even though they know it could kill them.

There is a question I have always wanted to ask. Why are francophone countries always raked by civil wars, and are so poor? Could one point the finger at the French? Remember Rwanda, Burundi, DRC, Central African Republic, and the list is endless. I am out of line here. After all, it's one's *self* that constructs the place they inhabit.

Abidjan is now littered with corpses rotting, and little kids kid soldiers are stepping on these corpses as they rush to a killing, diving into this reef of confusion. Grandmothers and mothers oyed and oy-veyed at the little ones playing big soldier mentality in the battle consumed streets.

It is so sick, sick, sick, sick, sick, sick....

Stations of the Cross

He is hitting my head, I am falling to the ground, and he is hitting me, again and again. He is grabbing my hair. He is pounding my head on the floor. He is shouting at me, scolding me, calling me "stupid", "dumb". He is pulling down my skirt and pant. He is taking off his belt, and pulling it into a loop. He is whipping me. He keeps whipping me. I feel like fire is shooting through my body...It hurts to sit for days. A week later, I am going into the church. There is no one in the church, but me. It is quite. It smells good- incense and candles burning. It is so peaceful. I walk over to the Stations of the Cross. I love Jesus. I think I know how he felt...at least a little. I cry. I feel very close to him.

1

The first station of the cross, "Jesus is condemned to death". My father keeps telling me he will kill me, even for small things like changing the channel of the TV!

This poem is for those who violate the conventions of human dignity
This poem is for those who violate the conventions of human freedom
This poem is for those who have cut budgets, closed schools
This poem is for Jonah who can't read and write
This poem is for Mathew who is deaf
This poem is for Maria who is blind

They taunted, tormented and teased them
It is a hate crime, the beast that never perished
It re-arranged into these cruel children's hearts

This poem is for children living in child labour camps
Farm boys, hands throbbing from the suns
Working the fields, with no school to go.
Because they are poor, because they are young
Brushing out the lamp of hope in their hearts.
This poem is for children who don't have food, shelter and hope
The weeping child, anguished cries that makes no sound at all
It is for children who know the deep throbbing vacancy of hunger
For food, home, love, space, light and stars that remember.

2

The second station of the cross, "Jesus bears his cross". I feel a heavy weight pressing me down....my father's presence alone in the house is a heavy cross for me.

At 10 days of age, I was shocked by the gunshots of my parents' voices, shooting at each other
At 10 weeks of age, Calvin was fed with Sadza and Mutowejongwe (salted water)
At 10 months of age, Mary was raped by her father to gain good luck
At 10 years of age, Jane was raped for the third time by our Maths teacher
Is God such a violent man?

3

The third station of the cross, "Jesus falls for the first time". When my father beats me I fall to the ground. He uses his whip until the blood flows.

Since age 11, Jane was refused schooling more than 11 times. Since age 11, Mary was used as a call girl more than 11 times. Since age 11, Jane was given in marriages, treated for sexually transmitted diseases. Since age 11, I was beaten more than 11 times. Since age 11, Mary was jailed in a juvenile facility 11 times. Since age 11, Jane was abducted, sold off to Angolan free labour workplaces 11 times. Since age 11, Mary was sold off to South African brothels 11 times. At age sixteen they were used up. They were just nothing, but a shell. They were released. They found their way home. They are now commercial sex workers. They are fallen angels, falling down… down…down, on their crosses.

4

The fourth station of the cross, "Jesus meets his mother". Once father beat my mother when she tried to refrain him from beating me, and now, she only watches- afraid of my father, or she doesn't love me anymore. Cruelty is like a flu bug, it is easily passed around!

This poems is for the pregnant girl with nowhere to go
This poem is for the boy in a cruel gang, learning the cruel nature of the world
This poem is for the child trying to make do in life

This poem is for the student called "stupid' who struggles in school
I see every day the increase of young beggars
I see every day the increase of illiterate children
I see every day the increase of unemployable young people
This poem is to kindle a flame of compassion

5

The fifth station of the cross, "Jesus is helped by Simon of Cyrene". I don't have friends anymore. I drive them away because I am always sad

This poem is for the raped girl trying to rebuild her life
This poems is for the teenage girl who is worried she isn't "pretty" enough
This poem is for the girl who hangs herself because of cruel words of others
This poem is for the teenage boy who lies about having sex and doing drugs
This poem should give you courage and hope to carry your cross
This poem is from God
This poem is for you

6

The sixth station of the cross, "Veronica wiping blood from the face of Jesus". No one wipes my tears for me, I am alone. Only God wipes my own tears for me.

God is for the ones terrified that this might be all there is in life

God is for the ones who wake up every morning without hope

God is for the ones who want nothing more than to be loved

God is for the ones who wonder whether they want to continue living

God is for the ones living this life alone

God is for you.

This poem is for you

7

The seventh station of the cross, "Jesus falls down for the second time. There is a day I thought he had finished beating me. I tried to rise up and run, but he started beating me again, I fell down again

God is for those who lost the light at the end of their tunnels

God is for those who have pushed far beyond their breaking point

God is for those broken beyond repair

God is for those suffering silently in the dark

God is for those fallen down for the second time

God is for those whose screams no one hears

8

The eighth station of the cross, "Jesus speaks to the women". My bed and I talk about father. We call him the devil. Sometimes we lean against the door while the devil is beating on the door, trying to get to me

This poem is for the ones who realizes not everything is their fault
This poem is for the ones who want to change the world
This poem is for the ones who imagine for a better world
This poem is for the ones who see hope where most people do not
This poem is for the ones whose minds are opened up by God

9

The ninth station of the cross, "Jesus falls down for a third time". After father beat me down, back on the floor, for the second time, I tried to get up, but I couldn't. I hurt too much and I fell back down for the third time

This poem is for the child of divorced parents who would always struggle
This poem is for the abused child who can never lead normal life
This poems is for the missing child who will never be found
This poem is for broken families whose pain is beyond comprehension
This poem falls down for the third time with you
This poem is for you

10

The tenth station of the cross, "Jesus is stripped of his garments". Daddy pulls my pants down to whip me

This poem is for the boy who feels striped by bullying at the playgrounds
This poem is for the child who plays video games all day
This poem is for the youths whose mind is corrupted by Hollywood and media
This poem is for the girl who only models because she thinks her body is all she has of value
This poem is for the child who has nothing to value in life
This poem is for those children who feel naked in their souls
This poem is for you

11

The eleventh station of the cross, "Jesus is nailed to the cross". When I am around father I feel frozen. I feel like I am nailed with invisible nails to an invisible cross. When he beats me, the whip is like the hammer hitting at the nails, the whip connecting to my body is the nail. I can hear it sounding off "gong, gong, gong", on my flesh. I can feel the pain, hitting the bottoms of my soul. I bled tears of blood from my soul. I feel myself dying, slowly.

12

The twelfth station of the cross, "Jesus dies on the cross". Father hurts me. I can't get away. I don't talk to anyone; I am dying inside my soul.

This poem is for tears no one hears
This poem is for voices lost in this translation
This poem is for voices that die in this translation

13

The thirteenth station of the cross, "Jesus is removed from the cross". When I remained on the ground, father yanked me off the floor, holding my hair. He dumped me on my bed, but I couldn't sit. My body is all wounds. I can't even rise myself, as he rapes me. I am powerless. I am dead.

14

The fourteenth station of the cross, "Jesus is buried". I am buried in a grave, I know. Like Jesus, I am a seed; I know one day I will leave it all. One day, I will reach the end of my tunnel.

This poem is for those waiting for a better tomorrow
This poem is saying we are all one in God
This poem is saying love is all we really need
This poem is saying, **"Stop child abuse!"**
This poem is for Mathew
This poem is for Calvin
This poem is for Jane
This poem is for Mary
This poem is for Maria
This poem is for Jonah
This poem is for you
And you
And you
And you...

The real nuclear threat

An earthquake, tsunami,
engulfing
plumes of smoke, smog.
threat, radiation threat 10 000
waters. Places that are over 1000
23 000 confirmed dead,
homeless,
missing trapped
intelligence
days their naked emperor,
the disaster area. Like caution
morning of first meeting, maybe
he was sure he didn't even have
Japan, at that. When he was told
radiation threatened
century when
else's little bundle in
Fikushima is worse
a now
we won't talk of
Especially not about Nagasaki?
5-9
threat,
the western world
that country...,
we begin
every of their sins...

and then a nuclear disaster
the skies with
Japan is now a
times more in its
miles away scare, over
thousands left
thousands are still
inside this cold
as close as death. It took 28
their prime minister, to visit
in the
he waited until
to run out of
it was safe to visit the
area. After all, this is the
we like death to be someone
an unknown country.
than Chernobyl 86, Russia, claiming
that history makes and records. And
Nagasaki and Hiroshima, no!
months to clear the radiation
and with what effects....why isn't
ablating the right or wrong of this or
to have nuclear capacities, until
to hate these sinners, loving

Ask Iran!

There are now numbed neutrons speeding to meet its atomic
horizons.

Sexually Transmitted Leadership

I will sleep with you if you can neglect your ailing wife for me. I will sleep with you because your wife would soon die. I will sleep with you if you show me where the money is. I will sleep with you if you show me where the power is. I will sleep with you if you allow me to sleep with other men, who will bear you kids. I will sleep with you as you rape the country, raze and plunder it. I will sleep with you as we gallivant in western capitals, in oriental cities. I will sleep with you for the clothes and jewellery. I will sleep with you and you and you...

I will sleep with you for my kids' future. I will sleep with you for my education. I will sleep with every professor of my studies. I would have slept with them had they improved my grading at that Western university, but they refused. So I slept with that Eastern University's professors to get my honours. I will sleep with you for the doctorate degree. I will sleep with you for the chairmanship of the League. I will sleep with you for the publicity. I will sleep with you as you support my candidature for the presidency. I will sleep with you as you vote for me. I will sleep with the whole country to vote for me. I will sleep with the orphans. I will sleep with the women. I will sleep with the youths. I will sleep with every rival politician to garner their support. I will sleep with you for the future of my kids. And then, my kids will sleep with you to positions and power. Their wives and husbands will sleep with you to positions and power. My grandsons and granddaughters will sleep with you for positions and power. Their wives and husbands will sleep with you for positions and power. And yes,…

In case a lot of you are still asking why I got my PHD in less than 3 months. The answer is: I am a Permanent Home Dweller.

What were my research findings?

"I was shocked all orphans in Zimbabwe have no parents!"

Caesar's breathe

Chernobyl is still a living thing, an evil, a dragon fire-breathing thing. A myth!

It emerges from its darkness now and then to consume food, to feed on anything it can reach.

Not only for food, but anything can invoke it. Then it will rise from the dead, like a bad-ass Lazarus?

Fire, wind, water..., then it spouts those bastard radionuclides into the air.

These little monster flies wherever they feel like going without care of borders, passports, laws, bloody governments...

It sprouted its ugliness ten years after 86. Contaminating on top of the original 135 000 citizens, another 3.7 million who stayed in areas of significant contamination.

The area extents from just north of Kiev, Ukraine to Mogilev, Belarus and as far eastwards Tula, Russia.

Its effects includes among other cancers, thyroid cancer in little children, radiation exposures, stress induced illness like high rates, abnormally high rates of heart diseases, alcoholism, suicide, crumbling economies and failed governments, the Soviet Union project? It has made both Belarus and Ukraine poor as they try to contain it.

Hundreds of billions have been drained, consumed by this monster, in trying to contain the monster's breath.

The rise in the water level of Pripyat river due to flooding, floods across, heavily-contaminated-with-radioactive-elements such as caesium 137 and plutonium, areas.

These particles are washed into the waterways that feed Kiev and other cities as far as Odessa on the black sea, blackening it all the more!

The concrete steel sarcophagus hurriedly elected in 86 to seal the reactor 4 is a threat to over 10 000 people who work and live nearby.

It is riddled with holes that allow rainwater to pour inside thus deteriorate support structures.

This structure can collapse any moment, sending up plumes of radioactive remnants afar.

Other dangers are the 15 similar reactors to the number 4 reactor that continue to operate in the former Soviet Union.

These unlike the ones which use water in generating a nuclear chain reaction, uses solid blocks of pure carbon(graphite).

It is highly inflammable and can propel a lot of radiation far out into atmosphere to even endanger our coveted place.

Heir apparent Europa is highly susceptible to a further Chernobyls.

The oneness, universality, or globality of the world is explained as "Caesar's breathe" by the literary gods.

The assassination of a leader, Caesar, and his breathe, his very last breathe, his final exhalation contained about as many molecules of oxygen and nitrogen as they are lungfuls of air in the earth's atmosphere.

Every breath that we take, everything that we do contains a molecule of the very air of Julius, the "Caesar's breathe."

If that's so think of Chernobyl 86, Fikushima 2011, and small many other nuclear disasters, traces of whose were detected as far away and as high above, and as deeper below!

I don't want to talk of the god-flash of Hiroshima and the Satan in the mantle of Christ, Nagasaki. The Americans don't want to talk about that, too. They were right; they always think they are right! But over 2 00 000 is unjustifiable. Maybe it was justifiable in that century of mad machine death.

But, it only means now and forever, every breathe we take will contain pieces of these deadly coughs.

Team Israel

Israel
Britain
Egypt
Christians
Jews
USA
Saudi Arabia
EU
UN Security Council
USA Allies
Unconcerned

Team Palestine

Palestine
Turkey
Syria
Christians
Muslims
Iran
Lebanon
EU
UN General Assembly
USA Axis of Evil
Unconcerned

28

The Middle East Game

The Jewish kingdom is there in the bible, a kingdom. Syria is there in the bible. Lebanon is there. Palestine, (Philistine, are they the same?) is there. The Persian kingdom is there. Turkey, so too, Egypt, remember the pharaohs, the most hated in the bible?

All these nations are still there.

A land of saints for this razored bleeding hillside: Israel is still the sun, only now a black halo. All around it the world seems to surround it and revolve around it. Palestine, the sheep at the altar; is where the games are usually played, the balls are the bombs, and the trophy is land.

Israel was formed in 1948 as a state, and invaded Palestine in 1967 after defeating the Arab armies which didn't want it to exist as a state, rather as a kingdom under Palestine. Israel also occupied Syria (the Golan Heights), and Southern Lebanon and Egypt (Mount Sinai).

After all, Moses told the Jews to "show no mercy" to everyone who was not Jewish!

And now, here is the revolved game: Syria supports the Hizhallah guerrillas in Lebanon who pummels Israel in this border area with bombs, thus stoking Israeli anger. Israel hits back on innocent Lebanon civilians, another sheep at the altar.

In doing this Syria wants Israel to leave her Golan Heights. Iran supports both Syria and Hizballah with military equipment, so also Hamas, and at onetime PLO's *fatwa*, they would carry bombs into Israel homes, buses and buildings, on their bodies, blowing themselves in these places, thereby killing innocent Israelis, stoking Israeli anger.

So, Israel blocks and imprisons Palestine, starving the Palestinian people to death, or just bomb them, or confiscate their territories for more Israeli settlements so as to make them accede to Israeli concessions on the negotiations table.

No, it's not a game. It is a bloody war!
The real tragedy of Israel is; it is imprisoned in its identification of race with right.

Egypt has been an accomplice, the guards in these open prisons Israel creates in Palestine, blocking Gaza residents from accessing food, or cover from the Israeli bombs.

In comes the USA: supplying and arming Israel with everything they need to fight their wars, and telling Egypt to toe the line. Israel gave up Mt Sinai to the Egyptians as payment for this accomplice.

Palestine wants its land back, in East Jerusalem, West bank and Hebron, Israel doesn't want to let go. Israel now says it has destroyed enough of Palestinian homes and replaced them with illegal Jewish settlements to make them Israeli land, despite many UN resolutions that disagree with this.

Syria and Lebanon wants its land back but Israel won't give it back without a peace deal. America is the referee, player and official... The whole world is either America's allies or its axis of evil. And then, the game continues...

Perpetuating 1967

There are parts of Johannesburg predominantly occupied by the Zimbabweans.
There are parts of London predominantly occupied by other races from other countries.
There are parts of the US that are occupied by say the Chinese, Koreans, and other foreigners.

What Netanyahu is saying is Zimbabwe has every right to confiscate parts of Johannesburg. The Jamaicans should confiscated Luton, in the UK. Korea should confiscate Korea town say in America. China should do that to many areas towns, cities, countries, continents, all over the world... That is the gospel of Netanyahuism, after all! Who is Netanyahu?

Netanyahu is a riddle
Netanyahu is a name
It is next to nothing
Nothing is Netanyahu
A name, his name
Netanyahu is a liar.

Across the road
I see an old house
It's a Palestinian home
Being torn, demolished

The bricks of yesteryear
Cluttering on the ground

Gathering on top of
Other bricks of yesteryear
Crushing and suffocating them
Such slaughtering significance!

Floating above this defeated air of another time among these
discarded debris, sharp intelligences becomes sharp choppers.
It is the slow un-dramatic amassing of history?

There are questions we never asked. And answers we never
want to hear.

Nazi Israel

Written in response to the destruction of the Sheppard hotel in East Jerusalem by the Israeli government to make way for a new Jewish illegal settlement.

We gaze again
enthralled, entranced
As Nazi Israel
destroy, decapitate
The Sheppard hotel

We gaze again
unconcerned, undecided
As apartheid Israel
deface, defile
East Jerusalem

We gaze again
par-taking, propping
As racist Israel
murder, mutilate
Gaza strip

We gaze again
rejoicing, recounting
As mad Israel
wound, waste
Arab Palestine

We gaze again
cackle, call

As recusant Israel
ravage, raze
Bright with hate!

i AM Going TO Marry HER

A boy, who thinks he is a man, and a woman who thinks she is a girl. One is in Harare, the other is in Johannesburg. He is Oedipus. He is like Oedipus. Oedipus is like Chaka Zulu. She is Mbuya Nehanda. Chaka Zulu is like Mzilikazi. Mbuya Nehanda is a man, like say, Tichakunda. Why didn't you marry all these years? You are now 40. 40 is like the new 30. 30 is like 20, 20 is like 0, the new 0. We get born at 20, yet some say life begins at 40. Bit by bit this ageing is the prey, he will feast on it. Zero is like a hero, at that hill. I was waiting until I mature, I was pursuing something else, and that is nothing. Nothing is something which is nothing. Iteration, and you are asking me what's going to happen, and I am saying it's already happening, like silent things talking in the dark. Mzilikazi is like king Makoni. Whose head, or is it skull, or whatever is somewhere like not here, somewhere like No(r)where(way). They took his brain to learn about how an intelligent African man thinks. He had made his own Chimurenga from his bode of Makoni, and they didn't know what genius drove this war thinker. Tichakunda is her boyfriend, her lover, and she has been trying to figure out how he functions, taking his brains into her heart. With heat she hopes to change her luck lustre, halt the continuing built of years on his frame. I am single and I have told her I love her when she was a burning thing on me, Tichakunda thinks. King Makoni is Lobengula's lover. The first job Lobengula had was taking down his pants and pee to an old man in Matopos hills, who lived near Rhodes' gravesite. It was easy money, steady work, and flexible hours. The old man never touched Lobengula, never frightened him. He just gave him money, a dime for every puddle he made. Lobengula was a

36

boy, in the shadows of his father Mzilikazi. And they say it's a western invention. Lobengula watched the Matopos sands turn dark as the hot liquid (puddle) spread. It felt good, very liberating, and he got his dime (to buy sugar), and he accepted it, and kept it as a secret, between him and the old man. Lobengula is like Nkomo (which one, it's not a question.), Nkomo is like Mugabe (Davidsons) David's son is like Z, is like Mbuya Nehanda, Mbuya Nehanda who is like Winnie Mandela. Winnie Mandela is like Mitchell Obama, and is that African. Osama is like Obama (not Winnie Obama). So, you are now ready to marry (me). Winnie asks Nelson, Nelson who is like Desmond. Desmond is like Robert. Robert is like Helen. Helen is my grandmother. Yes, I am now ready to marry (you) grandmother. Helen is happy, her drapes open up. Helen tells the good news bible to her AU-ntie Joyce. Joyce is happy. She is going to pick a fat cheque (Auntie's dowry). Joyce is like Joseph, the goat's face is like Pumzile, who is like Simon. Simon is like Thabo, who is like Jacob, who is like Cain, where the hell is that son of mine; I can feel he is trouble. Jacob is like Joshua (tree), like John, like Didymus, like Kgalema, like Emerson, like Morgan. Morgan is like Tendai, not me. I am like Tichakunda. I am going to marry her. And they offered him a scholarship to write a bio note about Davidsons. Does Davidsons work at ZESA, ZIMSEC, ZIMRA, ZEC, ZISCO, and Z…LAST? And they denied me my chance to write about (a novel, which is poetry) South Africa, 60 plus million years ago. They say they know everything from back then. I could have told them they don't know because they don't speak the language anymore. It was the world before voice, before the ape in you. Maybe I should have proposed to write this poem about Tichakunda and his girl Nehanda. I am listening to her favourite music, singer, Tracy Chapman, *across the lines…,* and who doesn't like Tracy. Tracy is a pickpocket. Tracy is like Celine, who is like Dolly, the sheep, who is like Whitney, who is like Bobby Mariah, who is like Madonna…not the painting from that mad painter. It's Picasso rather who painted it, so a kid could have painted it. But who doesn't like a bio note on Picasso, who is like Madonna, who is like Celine. But they are not African. African as Africa is for Africans, ask Davidsons. So what is Irene doing here? She told me I don't have talent. She said I am like Mbidzo, Mbidzo who is like Tsitsi, who is like Batsi, who is like Charles, who is like the-far-way, who is like Christopher, who is like Dambudzo, who is like Shimmer shimmering in the morning's sun like dew would. Mbidzo rhymes rhythmically, poetrically. But, I don't. Is this a poem? Irene whatever, whatever Irene, I mean whatever. Irene is right, which is correct, that I don't have talent. So, they were correct, which is right in giving him the scholarship to write about Davidsons who is Z, is like Z. I am the last one of my group at school to want to marry, so I must not have any talent, even for marriage. I will be the last one to marry. I have succeeded without talent, to even make someone think of it, to think of it, myself, me, I. At last, this time they did not recycle the winners, they vary in subtle, unimportant ways. It's getting such that it's a monarchy system, feudatory with its masters and servants and sycophants, and prescription (proscription, the dictionary says they are different) writing. This pork barrel pedagogy they are peddling is like selling a blanket bearing measles. Those who were the selectors, as like always, are from the same crowd who win prizes but do not publish books afterwards, or if they publish, it's always one book wonder…and they are so talented. At least 4 were not from the same country. I would rather (if they were going to be 4 winners) they would have come from South Africa this time. Me, Tichakunda, because I am HERE (go and debate this if you want) is included with my thesis on South Africa before voice, which is word…and I won't write in these words, in this voice, and the next one should have been Julius (a star sized mind of a moon sized man, knowing that he has a lot to say) with his apartheid this diatribe South Africa, this and that, the next one, would be Mongosuthu on Nelson's bio note, and Nelson would write Desmond's bio note. It's already sold out man! They are always messing us here, messing us there, trying to rectify here, messing that, rectifying this, rectifying that. The rectification is complete on our loyal disaffection. Let me write a bio note about them. Me and the 253 who were messed in June, me and the 100 plus messed in July, me and the 300 plus messed in November, that is December. Me. Me. Me, that is always like me, me, and me. I am going to marry her, to love her concretely. Today I almost wrote a sentence! Z is like Z, which is like ABC, which is like XYZ, and I can't unhappen what has happened. I am always caught in this cycle of loosing, and this is a curtained caterwaul. Now, I feel better.

The rush to own

I wonder!
Anything unusual
Someone wants to claim it,
                     to own it.
"I started it."
"I formed it."
"I thought of it."
"They copied it from me."
Don't forget I formed the mountains,
Oceans, continents, galaxies....
          "The Tunisian revolution,"
          "The Egyptian revolution,"
Iran likes the music these makes.
Calls them
"Islamic awakening,"
As if it formed them?
Such hubris! Forgetting.
They are Christians
In both countries.
It never was a matter of religion
But democracy.
"The Libyan war,"
The western wants
To protect the civilians
From Gadaffi
Wanting Gadaffi out. Amen.
Out-gaddaff-ing innocent civilians
For the oil! "Yemen revolution."
It ended up Yemen uprising.
                     Yeh man!

The tribal leaders against Selah.
Waiting for Yemen war?
Selah got lolli-bombed,
                    popped on his head.
By those tribalistic, thugs.
Got bandaged by those Saudis.
Mosque defecators?
"The Syrian revolution."
It's Assad cleansing games
Against his own people.
Assad calls them thugs,
thugging Assad, Owl-
            Bashir?
        "Bahrain revolution,"
It is those royal pagans
Against their own people
With the help of Saudi kings
Britain.
            Bahrain-ing the capitalist
World of business, Britain calls
Them
"The middle east revolutions"
'Anti government uprisings."
"Middle east disturbances."
Africa wants to refer to them as
'North African problems,"
Wants nothing of this on
Africa south of Zimbabwe,
Ask Zuma? And that's why
She likes to quell the Libyan war
Protecting her friend, Gadaffi
From the UN of NATO .

Thinking she is such a world power!
Israel and Saudi Arabia calls these
"Terrorist."
Or
"Dogs."
Or
"Thugs."
Or
....
It's the maddening rush to own!
Or

Infinity

Could infinity be demonstrated?
Using cause and effect.

Water could be the best way
to demonstrate it.

What is water?
What constitute it?

I am not talking of that scientific contrivance H to O thing,
no. It's not a good enough explanation.
There are both living and dead,
living in other contexts animals,
living in other contexts plants
in water, that will always
constitute water.

Water, can it really be lost.
Do we lose anything really?
It's been here.
It will always be here.

In mathematical terms they are infinities that can't be dealt
with mathematically like some quanta of energy that shows
infinity values. To solve them you have to do renormalisation,
which is the introduction of other infinites to solve or cancel
the first ones. In simple terms it means introducing a pest to
solve another pest, thus creating a new pest.

Some wars can be solved that way
Some cannot.
Some wars have too much infinity that can't be renormalised.

I can think of ethnic wars,
Israel-Arab warfare…
And wars between religions.
Moslems against Christians, Nigeria?

The holy war has been ongoing for years now...
Creating the third world war?

The effects of…
will
create
infinities
that can't
be solved.

Doing A Camus

Walk in front of me
But don't lead me
Don't colonise me
Don't boss me
Don't patronise me.

Don't walk behind me
I want someone to follow
I want someone to teach me
I want someone to push me
I want someone to revere.

If you walk besides me
You are a friend
You are a lover
You are a teacher
You keep me company.

Fundamentalism

The Moslems wants to conquer the whole world, until every person in the entire she-bang thing is submissive to Allah, through their warmongering jihads.

The few or so American infidels will be thrown into their hell.

The Christians wants to conquer the whole world. "All will be saved," is their war cry.

A few will have to be thrown into its hell after Jesus' second coming.

The question is which of the two is going to succeed? We only have one earth to do this. Which God, which heaven, which hell, is the question?

Maybe Buddhism, maybe Judaism, maybe time will succeed?

Buddhism and Judaism have the richness of the clock; they have forgotten they have to conquer the earth for them to be relevant. Have they?

Is this the "next Rwanda?"

Helicopters hovering\ roving\ round\ around\ loitering
hooligans.
Burning streets/ humming/ singing/ smoking/ angry…
choruses into the air
People being raped\ touched\ tortured\ hacked\ forced\
disappearing…
Children gutted, ----------- ------------ beheaded; an
oblation to machetes, AK47s, bombs, pangas, & chainsaws of
destruction…
6,000 to 10,000 boys & girls …tots,
totting, toy-toying
Forming part of these armed groups
belonging, owning:::::: it
Fanatics stampeding| stamping on| a civilian youth on the
head| stabbing him| stoning him… stones raining down on
his soft soil: gorging it| raining| rain raining| rivulets of red
water| watering| the hard soil
His body is dragged raggedly through the streets.
O, bringing back medieval France!
Soldiers look on @ this action movie; Jason
Stratham, transport me a tale! For this poem fails me;;;;;;;;;
& then dismembers me….. burned… **d….**

This war is a kind of a ⬚ ..building in which the
children asks when shall love, love/ love/ love/ love me….
arrive @ the front
door
And in another month, about **1,000** people are killed. I
said,,,,,,, killed!
Killed| killed\ killed/ killed| killed\ killed/ killed…..

This war is now a   beer hall in which adults (AU,
UN, EU, the fighters, men, woman, you, and you, and you…)
ask whether there is enough liquor   in the pantry to ensure
victory. Me, too!
Functioning on the territory of this squalid nation
                    Is   a   presidency   without   law,
functioning police   & courts?
Surely the other shoe will have to fall; falling ⌐falling ⌐falling
falling

The Séléka/ lekker north east/ rebels/ rebelling/ grouping/
regrouping/coup-ing/whooping/   for reprisal attacks\
attacking\ Anti-balaka\ unlucky\ rebels\ Christians
Anti-balaka/   barraging/   rampaging/   killing   Séléka
rebels   &   Muslims
Muslims   Vs.   Christians
in   Muslim areas.
Consumed by the doing/ doing/ doing/ doing…..
not by its meaning,
Christians   Vs.   Muslims
in   Christian areas.
The chaos in this landscape is complimented with harsh
particulars:
Muslims cannibalizing Christians, Christians cannibalizing
Muslims!
Bringing us to the discombobulated perception of our
surroundings
In this dangerous hour of forgetting, let us be careful of the
noise, which is rising to attack us with a lack of temperance
Let us not be seduced by the seraphim of more-
Unexplainable events!
Are their gold standards

Pushing history through space
In time we shall all return

The theory holds, tight as an atom

Is this the "next Rwanda?"

Bosnian Genocide's aftermath may be more apt

People are moving into religiously cleansed neighbourhoods.
Mixed in the permanence of blood, dirty and dusty
The sound wearing wind in its teeth is
Partitioning the Central African Republic into separate Christian and Muslim states

By May **2014,** it was reported around 600,000
Were internally displaced,
with 160,000
In the capital, Bangui/ Bangui/ Bangui/ Bangui…. I cry for you…. physique ruthless, a territory theory!
The Muslim population of Bangui has dropped from **138,000** to 900.
And a food crisis is looming! ♀

This Bangui shows me her new earrings |
lipstick | jewelry | fashionable clothing-
That distract/ detract/ intract/-able,
from the scars/scaring/ her cheeks
Revealing our paths\ roads\
bridges\ stations\

49

to ourselves & how to burn them down
No one knows for sure when Africa will actually
leave/ depart/ arrive/ stay///////
Herding for a new beginning we are forced to ponder|
listen| watch| not arrive:::::

Always making excuses
                    It feels natural, soothing like home
            A home where time hammers us into a place!

Every God

Every God for its uniqueness
Every God for its difference
To an individual
To everybody

Infinity and plurality of people
Infinity and multiplicity of nature

No single culture, no single flag
No single God, no single country

Utter embrace of every God
Every culture, every race
Every faith, every flag
Every country…

Karma's "shoe" list

~~George Washington Bush~~
~~Tim Howard~~
Watch out that flying shoe!
Tony Blair...

Undying echoes

A single beat of my heart
What did I see?
Continuous echoes of the beat
Resounding, on and on
Echoing, is it about the suffering
young and old?

Man waiting, crying for this-
a hopeless life
A country now mourning, weeping
bleeding into ruins.
In eternal seasons of darkness
as of the summer's rains.

A text for Haiti

It was not a rosy-fingered dusk, still light but darkening afternoon. That fateful day, that frightful afternoon is still a crazy dream. It was on 12 January 2010. At 16:53 in the late afternoon, dripping into evening, destiny knocked, like a birth of melancholy, carrying its elements into the streets

A furious, fiery, spiteful single beat of the earth
tracing her bloody legacy in agony
through dark Port-au-prince's darkened city
bringing the forgotten past of
1751, 1770, 1842, 1946
Flooring Port-au-prince, a Venice of the poor
and other listless cities tilting under
the weight, all gone flat
Jacmel, Leogane, and others
Whole towns that disappeared

Hundreds of thousands died an ignominious death, trapped like rats. Deadlocked, sandwiched between sheetrock, beams, crashed windows. Wrenched broken bridges across rivers and blooded receding streams of waters. Under astylar pavilions and stilted stucco, smashed cabins, roofing, reeling rafters

Dead bodies floating around
like bloated angels in saran wrap
The oil, stench, puke, shit, piss
gas, chemicals, an imperial alchemy
Oozing out and hospitals turned into
morgues, tents turned into hospitals
Open grounds turned into dormitories

A damaged kaleidoscope of the empty. Darkness flowing around you like a cloth draping one to the feet. A people at the loose ends. A country forgotten, dismissed, under the blistering cold winter nights, no warmth, no food. Tides of the poor, sick and hungry

All your hopes floating like soap bubbles
and pain becoming your very breath
A soul on nine tail lashings
the lashings, licking your soul
Crying tears, painful tears
tears of the depth
Tears of a divine despair
And when the crying is spent
You had to realise your wound Haiti

But here and there existential anger gave way to true and honest heroism. People, families, individuals pulling together. Their courage photographed and framed. Their voices, like voices of zombies, straight out of the collapsed buildings

Morti-vivants, rotting, living skeletons
Rescuing families stranded
Saving thousands of people
And I am energized by their voices
Zapped, I am carried forward

Haiti, I can only listen and hear the winds carrying random grave tides from miles that far away. Haiti, I know what I see cannot really be shown by the grief inside of you. Haiti, all that I can do is to slowly define it, to fit it to what you want

Haiti, it would be good to remember
and accept that not all storms
earthquakes, typhoons, tremors
are necessarily meant for you
Haiti, I know it is difficult to walk in this truth
When the child crying is your child.

Licking Wounds

like excess baggage to lands beyond
nutritious young men shipped daily to.
worlds-wild, of which they knew not
like wild beasts lived, like Lazarus, they
rolled boulders uphill all day long, eating out of view
rich man's little crumbs. lumps and left-over's
with volcanic aversion they were viewed

rumbling cloud of troops on troops, cattle, horses, carriages
across our vast and flowingly fertile homelands.
scrambling erupted, so did bloody dissection.
bequeathing unto their bloated bellies rich lands.
stretching beyond the reach of eyes
a sinner's harvest of; gold, oil, silver, ivory, looted
to enrich a people belonging, not from our mothers' wombs.
leaving a honeycomb, nectar-less, depleted

lowly tribal trust lands paired to dark ones
in townships, farm compounds, in prisons
in our own birth-right by a people ungrown from our soil.
sun kissed fertile highlands paired to light ones
as oceans-apart, divided we stood
like prisoners in chains, dark toiled for food
light harvesting milk: dark- tears and sweat
light took all of dark's tears and sweat
which they feasted on to enrich themselves

dark shrouded in shadow's enlightment.
light enjoying the river of enlightment.
dark exiled from enlightment to slave for light

light a rhizome of enlightment to master dark.
in unlit, dirt, potholed streets, dark
loitered, leisured, shopped, slaved
in streets like paradise's golden paved lands
light worked, ate, shopped, leisured

at war, dark against light, for freedom
were sacrifices both sides of the divide
cripples, orphans, casualties
resulting in strawberry saturated freedom
but in-came, another colour, light unlike
yet dark it remained, lied to dark
like a mosquito it cared little but sapped
continuously scrambling on a scale so shameless
taking all, eating all, sharing in nothing

in light the other people happily live
in darkness, painted by someone else's hands
we live and lick wounds still painful
What stink in our soul, called evils, flies in our core?
to deserve this slicing dismemberment of our ideals?
Can our cloudy eyes provide diagnosis-
to reverse the course of our rotting prognosis?
Can we re-read the pages of our past
to weave the dreams of our future?

Murphy's un-thought

How I wish for a falling toast
To land on the buttered side
Making me realise that it is 60 years
Since Murphy un-thought
"Murphy's law."

"Whatever can go wrong,
will go wrong."
And with what practical application?

The more I have fought for freedom
The further that I have been
Far from being free

But the other side of this
Might result in me being free
But I would rather not
For I am rabid optimist.

SOMALIA, "the death walk"

It's like souls, lost souls walking in the damp chill of the Hades. Little angels walking, as pained; the stomach of a starving child, hundreds of thousands of miles to food camps dotted in and around the horn of Africa.
Across to Yemen.

It's the Somalians. Facing again up to another problem, leaving their country, leaving in droves again. They are always leaving; it's now a part of their DNA. Such are the markers of meal times, leaving, leaving, leaving…

The want of nothing more; is it the simpler version? Of the most difficult of this long constant, hunger is a lifetime. Close to a million have left due to this hunger. There is always a war in the mix; the war is a lifetime, too. Remember the days of Samuel Doe, the subsequent killing fields. The years of Saide Barre!

Of the warlords, Farah Aidid! He pelted the Americans out in 1992. He was later gobbled. The country got divided, creating three kingdoms. Into these three kingdoms, every day of its life, it is dying.

It still exists, though. Three kingdoms that are dying, dying from an overdose of self destructive tendencies. It's in Southern Somalia; hunger and famine has hit the hardest! It is the worst drought in over 60 years.

Killing tens of thousands. Whilst mother UN and the whole world do their talkathon. Talking about talks! Not to forget the killings from the al-shabaab.
Those terrorist dogs?

Those bastards who control the biggest part of Somalia, Southern, killing, killing and killing... Kenya now hosts the biggest refugee city in the world. Bar Palestine of course! A home to half a million refugees; and the walks don't stop... Walking...

"When we are walking if a dog collapses and fail to rise up we leave it to die there. If a child collapses and fail to rise we leave the child to die there, too. We can't carry anything heavy whilst walking."

"How many children did you leave behind?"

"I left six children behind. I had eleven children, now I have five."

Six children, staying, unable to decipher, the patterns in their own eyes!

Untitled

Eat they eat
We only harvest

Lead they lead
We only follow

Titles unaccounted
They have

Unknown to them
Are some of their titles?

So much they have
So little we have

But how does it feel
To have no title at all

Euro burning

It started with Greece. The former Byzantium Empire. Greece re-conquered Europe again but with its problems....

It started by gobbling the Irish, then it conquered Portugal, and it still refused to be contained.

Next it would take in Spain, with its over 23% unemployment rate, then it would chew Italy (with 120% debts to its GDP), and it would swallow the beautiful Nordic, then Herr Europa herself, if it stays unsolved.

Herr Europa herself is still the un-sunk ship (yet). It is V.I.P part of the sinking titanic, and the rest of Europe has hit an iceberg, somewhere near Iceland which dealt with such things differently before. Maybe Europe might ask for advice?

A bit on the safe are the UK and the Nordic north, Switzerland, and others who have refused to enter this sinking ship, keeping to their adored pounds, francs, kroner...

The capital of Europe, Belgium has now existed without a government for over 13 months. It's a country without a government but it is doing well.

I think it is a cool proposal for Europe to think along the Brussels lines: no government, no debt crisis....
Now that is an idea!

The Shadow Now Gone

the curtains closed
a shadow so huge, terrifying, threatening
an open but silent mouth came
yet many have disappeared in its quest
the do-ones survived, so too, the dumb-ones
it's been ages we have been in this dark.

then the curtains lifted
light filtering to our eyes, thus exposing
the decay, the silence, the hurt, imposing!
the shadows started lifting and dissipating
now, the light to lead us, we have-
of a shadow now gone, no fear, no favour.

Fermi's paradox

The land so
sparse, unpopulated
Only to be fitted
with groans and cries.

"Where the hell is everybody?"

US grand political theatre

It has to raise the debt ceiling to 14 trillion against its GDP of over 15 trillion dollars. Don't sweat over the numbers, please! The fight in its house of congress is for this. It means the mighty US is just about a trillion or so worth in real terms, making it worth just about an average western European country's economy. Of this debt, 30% is owned by China, thus China owns a third of the US. Making it the richest country in the world! It means the 300 million or so Americans really owns a trillion dollars. The power hungry Russian Mafioso calls America an economic parasite. An economic terrorist is what I would call it. It has terrorized the world economy for some time now, not to mention the last three years. Its actors, the republicans and the democrats have made great political theatre with their "cut, cap and balance" versus "more taxes for the rich" games. Some Middle Eastern guru thinks it's simply a race to the bottom. Deliberately weakening of the American economy to bring labour costs to as low as their competitors like India and China so as to compete. Its unemployment rate is pushing up; the general people are becoming poorer and poorer... Barrack tries tact with a 400 billion dollar jobs creation package. The republicans want to nibble this biscuit slowly, enjoying its crunchy sweetness. They demand that the bill be passed and implemented part by part, through negotiations, haggling, thus creating another grandstanding political theatre for the entranced world. This wasteful job creation exercise will be another waste. Is this what democracy means, really? It's the people who will always get a raw deal. But, let's enjoy the free theatre in the meanwhile if we are not really American... after all we will eventually be the poorer for it tomorrow.

for the mullahs in Iran

We are husband and wife
contemplating each other
like ancient enemies, but
we are bound together.

Yet, there is no reflection of
love, that I find in your
eyes, when I meet your gaze.
Only the look that you don't
want to be me, a woman.
Only the owner's pride!

My life is now determined
with what I have down south.
Is it pornographic? It is limiting-
This black hole of gaping.

You want to keep me
Hidden, my voice silent.
Or a lot more shy, sometimes
even dead…

There is too much sense of
fear, I am living in fear
of a death sentence-
By stoning, hanging, or shooting.
Ask Neda Agha Soltan's bones.
So, I have cooled my fierce femininity
which is triangular and angry
but knows what it is worth?

I am half your worth
½ a person, so I live ½
as good a life.
I have to cover more than ½ my body in
a doek, whether I am foreign
or local, as long as I am a woman!

No short pants, no mini-skirt.
No snogling in the park.
No loving, if I am not tied to you.

I wonder?
Since a soul is a hermaphrodite-
Will I be the man, will you be
the woman, will we be
Androgynous.

Are you still going to decide
what's my worth.., my soul's?
worth, beyond the grave.

He Was Never Free

He wanted us to be free
Up and down our land
He fought for our freedoms
But he was never free
Chained by our dreams for freedom

They jailed him for 27 yrs
Inside chains, bars, cages, walls
Still fighting for our freedom
The beast they caged was never free
Inside these chains, bars, cages, walls

They released him in 1990
And for the next 4 yrs
He was never free
Still fighting for our freedom
In negotiations, disagreements, threats

In 1994, he said we were now free
In the land of our birth
But he was never free
Leading us from the brink to sanity
Avoiding confrontations, arguments, fights
Still chained by our need to find rooting

5 yrs later he wanted to rest from us
But he was never free from us
He was still our prisoner
Always asking for more from him
To free us from our own chains

In his ailing years, over the years
We refused him freedom
Enchaining him in hospital beds, tubes, pipes
Soft chains refusing him rest from us
Telling him he was still our prisoner
Telling God that our God still owed us

In death, he was never free
We held onto him as we made theatre out of him
For days on end we extolled about how he freed us
Moaning, chanting, praying, refusing
Him his dignity in his new home
Imprisoning him in our home

In casket, in soil, in heaven, in hell
He was never free from us
He wanted us to be free
He died for us to be free
But he never was free from us

Imprisoned in a grave, like a mosque
Temples that are shrines
We will visit, cry out our worries
Asking our God to free us
From ourselves, imprisoned
In the walls of our minds

He is a God we ever wished for
A God never professing he died for us
A God we expected everything from
A God who accepted our homage
A God who owes us ourselves

A God never free from us

Syrian Unrest

Assad is a haunted animal, chasing his people's pain and suffering to build his own strength. Short and stocky is the peasant's brutality! He has made a bit of some hoodwink reforms to please the Syrians, clutching at puny parallels, but they didn't bite it. These are the discourses of this fool with his unpalatable truths: He says there will be municipal elections in January 2012, and parliamentary elections in February 2012, but nothing about himself (the presidential elections), as if the protests have been about something else. Such innocence! Is not an option, Assad. You must die in your infancy. It doesn't matter you have only done ten years or so. That you are an infant as compared to Selah, for instance. Such innocence is not even an option in ageing, in decisions. It must die now. The west has entered into its usual games, eyes always miscalculating. They want Assad to dissolve. They say crimes contested by Assad are his crimes. The east, China and Russia group supports him, making him feel he has to keep bombing his people until they let him be. The east wants the reforms to be given a chance. The world now wrangles around these camps. The west enhances its position by throwing more sanctions (humanitarian, trade and diplomatic) pressure. The pressure mounts with the Arab league getting involved, butting in by slapping Assad with punitive sanctions. What's left is for the west to butt-in the Libyan way. The stage is ripe, with more and more Assad soldiers defecting to the people's cause. Are these another bunch of revolutionaries that will topple Assad, like what happened to Gadaffi, that fringed phylactory bound son of a prophet…?

Russia and China still refuse to authorise the imminent invasion through the Security Council vote. So Assad tramples his people's bleak efforts underfoot with his elephant foot. But the people are unmanned by fear. It means it's the Syrian people who are the buttered ones, the bludgeoned ones, the shattered ones…, stories turning into blood on their placards. Some are now preserved in clay peat, have a nose about their neck, their bodies and flesh now nourish the soil, and their ash makes up the dust.

We had no right to be there

Even the patriotic Bob Dole
didn't think they should have
invaded Vietnam, in the 60s
Read "Saigon," by Anthony Grey.
He thought so too, so did the Britons
The poet Terry Hetherington
inspires me.

We shouldn't have been there
That's now in Korea, the Americans
The British were still in
the colonial fields in Africa
Asia and the Americas.

In Cuba, no kuba for you
Battle of the figs, Kissinger
was he supposed to be there?
Fidel's beardo asks you?
In his communist lands!
Looking for what America, terrorists?

In the horn of Africa: America
Do you remember those
couple of weeks, days, a
month? Where you
supposed to be there.
In Somalia!
Pirates or Warlords?

Britain fell down in Kabul
in another century
A century later in Kabul, they
are still there. How about
Iraq; it's an emotional subject!
But where are the weapons Bush?
Blair? Britain is still asking you.

But why is it that it's only
afterwards, after being
where you are not supposed
to be, when you realise
You were not supposed to be
there, so where next…?

We don't need another war:
NOT IRAN!

no, no, no, no…
we don't need another war, no,
not Iran, no, no no.
leave Iran alone,
no no no,
not another war,
not another war,
not another war.
we don't need another war,
we don't need another war,
we don't need another war,
no no no,
not Iran, not Iran, not Iran,
no no no.
we don't need another Iraq,
we don't need another Iraq,
we don't need another Iraq,
no no no,
not Iran, not Iran, not Iran,
we don't need another war,
we don't need another war,
we don't need another war,
no no no,
not another Afghan,
not another Afghan,
not another Afghan,
no no no,
not another war,
not another war,

not another war,
no no no,
not another Libya,
not another Libya,
not another Libya,
no no no,
we don't need another war,
we don't need another war,
we don't need another war,
no no no,
not another war,
not another war,
not another war,
not Iran ,not Iran, not Iran,
no no no,
not another war,
not another war,
not another war,
no no no, no no no,
not another Iran,
no no no, no no no,
no no no, no no no,
no no no, no no no.....
we don't need another war.

An enemy inside

He is at it again. He is back in the bushes again, killing...
He always kills to survive. It is something deeper. He has entrenched this in his followers. The party always kills to survive. When it fails to find an enemy outside, it looks inside. It conjures an enemy inside. An enemy has to exist inside or else the party will die. Every time he is on the ropes, he creates a victim's posture for himself and the party. Everyone is an enemy. Everyone has to come forward, to profess their new allegiance to him to be spared. If you voice against him, or the party, if you are as little reluctant, if you remain silent, you an enemy. You have become an enemy. It is the victim's mentality that rules.

They borrowed it from the liberation war. The party borrow it every time they are on the heels. They use it. They are using it, now. Making us believe they are still victims, of whom, of what...

The Americans are the masters at that. Every generation creates its own enemies, existential enemies. Allowing the Americans to go to war. Could it because they still feel bad they couldn't compete in the First World War, or entered World War 2 late. Maybe it goes back to their civil war, maybe war of independence, definitely the colonial wars it fought against its enemy from the inside, the Indians. You know the America I am talking of! All these created Korea, Vietnam, Cuba, Somalia, Iraq, Afghanistan, and Iraq again, Soviet Union, Iran, North Korea..., each generation demanding its own war. Got its war, fought its war, never learning how to unlearn not (never) doing that again.

And they are at it again. Not the Americans, who are always at it, no. Him, and his party. Back into the bushes, but it's in the midst of us. In our Mbare, in our Mpopoma, in our Sakubva, the cleansing has taken root. Anyone against him has to go. As we head towards the Congress, what has been endorsed in our first family home, our spiritual home, has to pass. It is the woman of the house who is on the rampage. She has created mercenaries, too, like the husband. These mercenaries are working flat out, silencing any dissent against his plans, the party's plans; his party's plans. For it can only be his and his alone, otherwise they won't be no reason to create scapegoats in the party. Anyone against the creation of the monarchy that he started creating with our independence has to go. He is the president for life. He is the head of this monarchy. It is time to prepare for the future of his children. Kabila (wasn't he killed to make way for Joseph) sacrificed himself like a sheep on the Alter for his son. And Joseph is now the new Promised Land for the DRC...

2, 5 years of Obamania(less)

He hasn't closed Guatenamo bay. He hasn't stopped the interrogations of terrorist suspects in other countries. He hasn't stopped, stilled the economic depression, despite trillions he has splashed into the US economy. He is still haunted by a spearing US debt crisis, a child of Bush. He has simply nursed it into more potency. He hasn't stopped the wars in Iraq and Afghanistan. He has created his own wars in Libya, Yemen, Pakistan, Somalia etc..., against terrorist? He hasn't helped the Middle East pro-democracy movements much but the dictators. He has no solution to the Middle East game (Israel-Palestine issue). He has now been gobbled into the American, warmongering machine. He is like bush, only a softer Bush, and a more talkative Bush. He talks better than the stupid Texan farmer. He talks un-solutions into solutions...

Nobel Prize 2009

I will have to take the Nobel from you
Barrack, Morgan should have it.
He did better than you, Barrack
I like you very much, Barrack
I think you talk better than Morgan
So you talked yourself to the Nobel
And Morgan talked himself to Robert

I will have to take the Nobel from you
Barrack ok; I have to take the money
And give it to the victims of cyclone Robert
Morgan knows them very well
I will let them have the monies, at least
For exhuming and reburying of their dead

I will have to take the Nobel from you
Barrack, I will give it to Morgan
Morgan is a victim of cyclone Robert
Don't you think at least he deserves something?
For the bandaged and swollen head he got
From the cyclone's demented winds in Harare

I will have to take the Nobel from you
Barrack, I would rather George and Tony
Or even the dour Gordon have it, Barrack
At least they helped Morgan to tame
That destructive beast in Zimbabwe

I will have to take the Nobel from you
Barrack, I promise I won't give it to AU
I won't give it to SADC, the UN
I promise I won't give it to South Africa
No, I will only give it to Morgan.

Did George beat you up, maim you, Barrack?
Attempt to jail you, detain you and kill you?
Did George kill your wife, your grandchildren?
Starve you to death; kill your children with cholera,
Make your children become refugees.

I will have to take the Nobel from you
Barrack, ok; I know you love the recognition
But do you feel you deserve it, Barrack?
Don't you think I deserve it too, Barrack?
At least let Morgan have it, Barrack, please!
Don't you see he doesn't have anything now?
The cyclone took everything from him.

REVOLUTIONS: The sparrow's fall

That animal has reared its ugly head again, gobbling…. It is
about to swallow Gadaffi. He is surrounded, cornered,
like
a small rat. He thinks he is bellowing orders but he is
crying (that he will continue fighting until death, a martyr?).
The
red heat in his eyes! He is alone fighting for his Libya.
A
Tripoli that no longer exist, only in his fallow
imaginations. He is about to follow Bennali, Mubarak, the
Japanese prime
minister into this gobbling monster's stomach. He
thought
he was so invincible all those years. When he was
brother man to the revolutions in far flung parts of the globe.
Selah and
Assad will surely follow, until the monster is sated. It
will
swallow Saudi Arabia, Bahrain, Iran… There is always
one antidote to this monster; it is creating another monster of
the
same making. Gadaffi overthrew a monarchy through a
revolution (1969). They called it a bloodless revolution.
His revolutionary forces took over from Idriss and ruled
Libya for 42
years. Now another revolutionary force is
overthrowing
him. I think it should be time-up for these revolutions.
There is this need to break this circle. Revolutions have been,
in

the long run, refractory to democracy. Is this revolution
  going to be another monster, or a band of angels just
gunning for Gadaffi. He can't even decide which way to
  run…

The king's burden

The moon and stars hidden
in the clouds. The wind asks
for my totem. The colds asks
for identity papers, a policeman
patrolling the streets. The sun
has gone to sleep. Crickets making
music, asking each other for cigarettes
... In an unknown language I am.

The bird that has forgotten to
store some berries. Thinking the
Berry tree will always provide
berries. Saying, "If I eat today, then
tomorrow is the king's burden."
Now there are no berries on the tree
for the bird.

Is The Remainder Of The Way So Long

Darkness, ... dark,
It's too dark to see.
I never know where I stand,
Fall, ...all this tumultuous fall.
Moving,
Maybe all.
For how long have I been holding onto?

These circles-
On, odd and old,
They grow!

This dark night.
This long night-
Never ceasing!

What day,
What life-
That no longer shines.

Not so long ago,
Some day-
Years gone!

All those gay playthings,
Laughing,
The sun shone.
When there was so much light and love.

Those days!
What happened?
For them to change,
All of a sudden.

Spring's green hope,
Summer's rains-
Their care!

All that faith!
All the rains!
And everything alive.

Was it on a cloudless autumn day?
What..., with all that browning?
Trees and grass frowning.

Why can't I reach that light?
It can't be far?
Is it?
How far?

This haunting silence,
Serene-
Insane.
I tread along and carefully feel,
For the pathways and ledges to hold onto.

Until when, shall I be walking in this lane?
I could feel a change not so far my reach.
When will I reach that light once more?
Is the remainder of the way so long?

Gadaffism: Gone.

Gadaffi is gone, biting a bullet in his hometown. He was captured alive, but some zealous NTC thug (national transitional authority, the eastern revolutionary forces) gunned him with one bullet. To think that it just needed one bullet all along to save Libya. They dragged his dead body through the streets, blooding the streets, like a criminal. It reminds me of medieval France (13th century), where treason was paid for through being dragged alive, naked, in the streets, before the hang man's noose finishes the job. Such sweet thuggery, in Libya 2011, is a stoking thing. To think that the bustard that used to threaten everyone who didn't agree with him in his radio messages, was now just blood, stupid, uninteresting piece of carcass (meat), being dragged through Libyan cities, being viewed on the Tele? Yes he was a criminal, yes he deserved death, but WE wanted to enjoy his suffering like we are making soaps out of Mubarak's trials. But we (are we that civilised?) are being denied that. Maybe it doesn't really matter. He had to die so he died. It is now time to move on, together, or separately. We have to move on. We need

the elections, the constitution, democracy, not another gaddaffism. We still have a lot other gaddaffis to deal with all over the world. I hope they now know what eventually awaits them. I hope they are scared.
They have to be afraid. Be very, very afraid
you, Gadaffi. Hey, if you pass him in the
streets, tell him he is the next, that he
should be afraid. We are coming
for him. It will surely
happen!

Autumn

Forward to a rust reddish autumn
An orgy of layers, dancing mosaic paths
Emblems of our archetypes

And raging metaphors
of our times
Unthinkable parameters
If colours could swap?

Revolution re-focussing

I think it's time the whole world should start focusing on the
important issues affecting the millions who are in real
need.
Remember the Haiti disaster. Over 1000000 (Like
those
zeroes on the Zimbabwean currency) people are
still
refugees in tent cities with nothing much coming
out of that promised help, of over a year ago.
There are hundreds of thousands in Pakistan still waiting for
help after the tsunamis. There are hundreds of thousands
from Fikushima disaster still waiting for help in Japan.
There are millions of refugees in the Gaza Strip,
imprisoned by the Israelis without any
progress as to talks of their liberation.
There are now millions starving
to death in Somalia from hunger and unceasing warfare,
millions fleeing the Boko Haram madness in Nigeria.
Contrast
this with trillions and trillions wasted on Iraq,
Afghanistan,
Libya... On a people who were not even facing any
kind
of colossal extinction, death, threat, but dealing
with
dictators created and recreated by the
pugilists in these conflicts.

It took a Judas

I am going to show them; them humans a lesson. I will be an Adam making our world new, again. I will tell them: In their bible stories, like sunbeams, one of us is preparing for what might be the last day on earth so that the humans will have their sport, their fun, their ivory. It's not ours to choose what we want to do with our body parts. They need to take a step toward us…they have to include us. What I will do is when one of those humans comes to rescue us from other humans. With their guns, their speeches, their songs, their poetry. That someone still remembers us amaze and alarm us. There are vultures haunting on the towers of useless noise. But I am going to ask for an audience with the people, or for the right to express what we think, what we feel. It took a Judas to save the people so I will be a Judas for my fellows. I am going to ask them that instead of their poems, their stories, their sermons…, they allow me to demonstrate their cruelty. I will ask that an innocent harmless child be cut on his nose, or have eyes gorged, or mouth hacked off…. A tide of good works finding a level in this parallel world. I would thresh the air with the heft of my tail. My voice copied to poke fun, I will tell a joke at their expense. I will trade these human pieces, like the left-overs from an angels' party, to the lions for our own safety. I will ask humans how it feels to have a body part removed from their bodies, or their babies' bodies. To have tears, pain, and grief that trip the light fantastic, distortion that becomes reality, how to deal with that kind of pain, how is it possible someone can do that to someone, or something like that without conscience. This is what I will ask them to do rather than hearing the same poems, the same songs, the same sermons…. I will tell them, this is as right as rain.

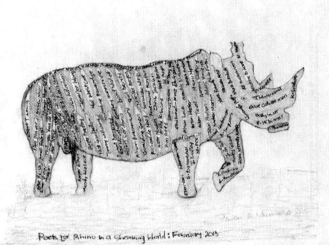

Poets for Rhino in a Shrinking World: February 2013

Bahrain/Yemen/Saudi Arabia- the music of the triangle

The Germans sells billions' worth of arms to the Saudis.
The British sells billions to the regime in Bahrain and Saudi.
US sell billions of arms to Yemen.

The Germany's arms are used to prop up the Saudi monarchy and on the pro-democracy uprising in Yemen and Bahrain. The British arms are used in Bahrain against innocent civilians.
The American arms are used against Yemen civilians.

These western powers talk of democracy as if they really believe it. Where is the sacrosanct right to democracy for the Bahrainis, Saudis, and Yemen people?

Where is the democracy for the Saudi woman who isn't allowed to drive in the streets, who isn't allowed to vote in elections?

Where is the democracy for doctors and health workers who were sentenced to over 15 years for treating people who had been maimed in the protests in Bahrain? Where is the democracy?

Where is the democracy for those who now anoint a green lane, a mountain top, a brook in Yemen, Bahrain, and Saudi Arabia with their remains?

A text for Baga

115 000, 20 000, 11 000, 5 000, 2 000
115 000 refugees out of Nigeria
Carrying with them black barrels of sadness
20 000 refugees out of Baga
Carrying the distance from what they loved most
11 000 of the 20 000 left for Chad
5 000 found their way to just outside Baga
Carrying their grief into a hundredfold of grief
2 000 extirpated in Baga and Dolan Baga
My grief cannot translate this beyond words
I would have loved to fly, howl and sizzle
Instead of this meagre mundane fizz

It felt like absence, it felt gone
2 000 wiped off the land, glutted, gutted, gunned
Like a loosening of the human sphincter
Into a river, an ocean of red blood flowing off
Bulleted blood pouring into Lake Chad
Vegetation, soils, ditches, stones, grass
Reddened; coloured red by an insane painter
In the name of religion, this insane painter kills
Maim, detain, rape, and kill again, displace, without care
Leaving tapes of grief flowing, tapes and tapes of it,
Flowing out, all human shit flushed out at once!

3 700 razed structures in Baga and Doran Baga
By the madness that descended on 3 January 2015
And for 4 days this God killed, injured, displaced
Made us sick; we lost our families, properties, livelihoods
Using fear to make us conform to its teachings

This God has a name: **Boko Haram**

We have called out to it before
Asking it to bring back our girls it had abducted
It brought them back strapping bombs on their little bodies
Burning us in its hot intelligence, fear and anger
Killing thousands all over our motherland
We have tried to stop calling for our babies back
Silently we have implored it, "Don't bring them back."
Not those ones who were coming back!

But the bullets never stopped flying our way
For the creation of a hard line Islamic state
In the north, north east Nigeria, it now controls
Killing over 2 000 in a small town!
This God killing civil vigilantes aiding the military?
This God doesn't care whom it would kill
And we can shout from our safe zones south
War crimes and crimes against humanity!
It doesn't bring them back, stop this killing God
The gulf between us sweeps breath across absence

A 50 year old running into the bushes
Dodging the red bullets, flying his way, says,
"I saw over 100 people being killed in Baga."
Another says, "Bodies were everywhere I looked."
Another says, "They were bodies decomposing in the
streets."
Another stepped on dead bodies for over 5 kms
Another says, "Over 300 young woman were taken for
amusements."
Another saw little children being gunned down

The pain of this powerlessness!

Half the body of the boy was out
Groaning red prayers
Breathing the hot angry smell of death
As bullets gutted it, pummelled it, and its mother
Killing a woman in labour, she died
With her unborn child
Death became the last word in human life
The last one in the shipwreck of humanity

It is all a cheat code
A God who kills to be worshipped
Doesn't care to kill itself; the unborn child
Who would worship it if it kills the innocent?
Who would be left in this killing field?
To worship it, to give alms to it, for it.
Who would care to love such a God?

My own maps are useless and invisible
This poem's inability to say what I want it to say
Your own editing of this draft of grief
A death without an echo, it means nothing
I am afraid to fall in love with this sound
The sound that can't be quieted
Of my own tears and their shapes
Yet we can only harmonize together in our soft
Braided chorus that sings of an ocean of grief

ECB vs The Federal Reserve:

Dead wood institutions.

Dead wood, reminding me of the Breton woods institutions: the World Bank (WB) and International monetary fund (IMF). These dead wood institutions' leaders of which are shared between Europe and the USA. It's a given that they are always headed by nationalities of these continents. Ask that Mexican central bank enthusiast! Another dead wood institution, European Central Bank (ECB) can't even buy bonds, can't do budgeting, can't create employment, and doesn't have any political powers. The powers still lies with the countries making up this entity EU. And the politicians are wary of making unpopular decisions, with their own electorate. So they don't always make the necessary decisions but try to talk the problems out. It figures that Merkel and Sarkozsy have had endless talkathons about the debt crisis in Europe without solutions to proffer. And the next line of dialogue waits in place with bated breath. The Federal Reserve Bank (USA) can buy bonds, can create jobs, and has political clout, but it still needs the approval of the politicos to work on any of these. Thus, it is a dead wood institution. Because the political machine in the US is a theatre, full of suspense (expense). It's always gamesmanship there. The Democrats versus the Republicans, other dead wood institutions? Decisions are always deferred, especially in election years. 2012 is election year so nothing is being done to save jobs, rescue the economy, create wealth and jobs for an average Joe, not Joe bidden. So the whole world watches as the two biggest movers pushes the whole world into another recession in the coming year. 2008 is just yesterday into our memories!

Squatter slums

The not-yet-in-the-now
The slums are still ghosts
Of yesterday, the slums we never
Left, demarcating boundaries of
Safe travel for comma travellers
Blinded, convulsing against mindsets

At home electricity was cut
In the dark of the candles' flame
We chew our nails, entertaining ourselves
With smells of kerosene fires, dampening
Our minds, sometimes eating cold
Bread, heavy and stale, too much butter
Tightening the vein that circled
Our throats, the cold drinks

We sleep in cold rooms
Getting warmth from the cold
Bodies, penetrating the night
Clawing the night's air
We have done away with sleep
Trying not to break
Trying not to crash
But still crying ourselves
Into child-eyed dreams

Freeing ourselves from the tyranny
Of facts, flying is just another
Embodiment of human exchange
Like fluids to language, currency

To meaning, sound to touch
I will name my unconcieved child
Hope, her hopes like morning dew
Will float like soap bubbles

Circling the cold air like streams
Of oppression, skin flying
The layered earth's flies
Singing sings of mother earth
Till we find ourselves again when
Slave becomes master, he will not
Rule us by force, by favour, by
Fear, he will not cage our hopes,
Our dreams in prison, his power
Will come by bestowing it on the
Brave and the beautiful in heart.

CORPORATISM vs. PEOPLE: occupy Wall Street

Not so long ago it used to be: there were four wheels of a car,
       available for the car. The executive, the judiciary, the
              legislature, the media. Each of which would jostle to
                     serve the car. The car being the people. Now it
is the
                            executive, the judiciary, the legislature and
the
                            people. The car is now big business.
The
                     world is now a school for Big
business.
                            Occupy Wall Street is a reaction of
the
                     people against big business, trying to
prise
                     big business's fingers off the government.
To
              strop their claws against this density of things so
that
    the government would return back to its mandates: to
care for its people, to create wealth for its people, to create
jobs for its people, health care, social welfare, to stop the
scrambling wars big business always sell and push with these
governments. Revolutions all over the world
are a direct response to this. America's
occupy Wall Street is a capstone to
these revolutions. All over
America, ordinary people
are in the streets, raising up against corporatism, fighting their

own government, its big business, the Wall Street.

Something is now happening all over the world. It's a happening thing that talks. The call is for a paradigm shift, to change the way we have been governed. The roof of time that covers this moment says: "Capitalism has failed. Democracy is now just a shell of what it used to be about. Religions are a bore." The whole world has caught wind of this.

It is happening in over 80 countries, over
hundreds of cities. It has whacked
London several times, devastated
Berlin, licked Paris, mesmerised
Sidney. From the far east,
to the far west. From
the far north to the
far south, and in
between it
sizzles…

The benched refugee

I have decided to say the story
But am I not too late?
Misunderstood by our own leaders
Unwanted by the other people
Pushed away by both

I am a Zimbabwean in South Africa
I am a South African from Zimbabwe
I am now in South Africa
Hyphens divide, so also
A leaky border

And every time there is a crime
He has to be a Zimbabwean
That's always the clue
But don't we pay good taxes
To keep you
To stay you from a sentence

But seizing us upon a minute's
Sprint is the creature intended to
Kill, built on hate and
Conformity, diversity and
Individuality unwanted

I don't want to be you
I want to be free to be me
I am neither fish nor fowl
I am the benched refugee
You have invented as a secret cave.

Bibi Aisha of Afghanistan

At 8 years old/
her father promised her hand/
in a marriage/
along with a baby sister/
a practice called "Baad"/
It is the law of the Pashtuns/
(in Pashtunwali area)/
to settle deputes between rival families/
At 16 she was handed over to her husband's father/
and brothers/
who were members of the Taliban/
in Oruzgan province/
Her husband was off fighting/
in Pakistan/
Tortured and abused by the family father/
and brothers of his husband/
she run away/
Two female neighbours promising/
to help her took her to Kandahar province/
where they wanted to sell her/
to another man/
They were stopped by the police/
and imprisoned/
Aisha as a runaway/
she was a woman/
A 3 year sentence was reduced to 5 months/
by Karzai (president)/
Eventually her father-in-law found her/
and took her back home/
She met her husband/

for the first time/
who took her to Taliban courts/
for dishonouring the family/
and bringing shame/
The court ruled the husband had to cut her nose and ears/
which he did in the mountains of Oruzgan/
He left her to die there/
but she survived/
Now she is an 18 year old woman/
with a cut nose, cut ears/

Pretty this grief

In the prisons of their minds
They float away on a river
Of denial

They dream of murdering
Their spouses
Before they are murdered

Drown their birth-ones in
Quicksand lake
Before they are drowned

These circling rivers of
Despair dangling
Chains that binds them
To life

It is a grief their patience
Was made for
They pretty this grief
With this reasoning

Terror war: through the eyes of Bush and Cheney

The unhinged Dick and dauphin George, despite an explicit
terror warning from the CIA in August 2001, failed to
protect America on September 11 2001, thus they
overreacted due to guilty and humiliation
of
failure. Star-matter they
created
their own purposes.
They
authorised
the torture of
suspected
terrorist for years, even
when there was no
imminent threats. They concocted
protection for themselves and other war
criminals in the administration through stupid
memos. Cheney and Bush set up torture networks of
interrogation cells where terror suspects were assaulted,
stretched, deafened, frozen, beaten, hung from
shackles.
Cheney, personally authorised water-
boarding of
prisoners, at least 183 times,
declaring it
as "just a splash of water"
on the
face, even though
pentagon

110

                                    conceded
                              several prisoners
                          were tortured to
                    death. The
            CIA
        found the
results of torture unreliable and
      sought to end it. Abraham
            Lincoln's habeas corpus (the
                    suspension of which for a short period) was
                          subverted into the total
                                presidential powers
                                      (dictatorship),
                          in a war
                          situation that was
                    unending. Bush,
                        through this Cheney device,
                  violated the law with
                    impunity, without a whisper of guilt
          and
              accountability, like an unhinged
        thing, killing close to
    a million Iraqis,
    putting
thousands
    of soldiers
        on death's
            row from the al-
                Qaeda's, losing the
                    country trillions, bankrupting
                          America and the whole world.
                            Creating this pervading,

permanent tone of
belligerence
and
unflappable
infallibility in
American
leadership.
America has failed to
shake off this Bush-Cheney
image and rules of engagement with the
entire world.
They never concede they were wrong, ask Iraq
about those purported weapons of mass
destruction that so far haven't
been found in Iraq,
never conciliatory,
ask Iran and
North
Korea,
never reflect, it
always create stupid
wars like Korea,
Cuba, and
Somalia...
In a war
situation if
you
fail to follow
rules of engagement
like
what the likes of Samuel
Taylor, Slobodan

Milosevic, and Radovan Karadzic
did, you should be
brought before the international law.
The question we must learn is when the
likes of Bush, Blair, Brown and Cheney
will be brought before the law for war crimes and
crimes
against humanity?

Saying what's already said

His mouth climbs up to his nose.
His teeth doesn't know the wind
And when he opens his mouth.
He peppers words full of honey
and poison, words that finds death.
He wants them to die. He lets them
Kill each other. What kind of a person?
Who drinks his own blood?
Is his own tick, a vulture...

Killing what he can't even eat
He is a leopard, a snake
It circles his heart, he fights it
Like bees. He is an army, no
talks. Talking about talks
he stands up. You tell him this truth
And he says you are joking. You are
saying what's already said.

That you can't play with clay
where there is no water; that if you
kill someone. Beware of Simon's axe
That you can kill a cow; a person
There is no refuge. His blood
will sit on your homesteads. Your
homesteads will be surrounded
by graves.

What's in his heart? It is a cave
His heart is his own blanket

He sleeps in. And to thank the dark
is for him to thank the things
he has come up with in the dark
Before he has arrived
He knew what surrounded
him, and he is now too late.

Drone Attacks

America now has the solution. For years, decades, centuries, it has lost its sons in foreign war adventures. Remember the 50000+ lost in Vietnam. Those lost in Korea, the World wars, Cuba's battle of figs, Iraq, Somalia, and Afghanistan, its civil war. So it has decided to spare its sons.

It bombed (droned) Iraq to rubble.
It bombed (droned) Libya to rubble.
It bombed (droned) Afghanistan into rubble.
It bombed (droned) (is still bombing) Pakistan.
It is bombing (droning) Somalia.
It is bombing (droning) Yemen.

It will bomb (drone) Iran.
It will bomb (drone) north Korea.
It will bomb (drone) Zimbabwe.
It will bomb (drone) Russia, china, Cuba…
It will bomb (drone) the whole world into rubble without losing not a single tear or sweat, or even a single cell of blood.

It will control the world from anywhere in the middle of the vast American Midwest, deep south, east coast, west coast, north coast…

Whilst our best multilingual grins ignores any lingering sense of displaced grace!

Printed in the United States
By Bookmasters